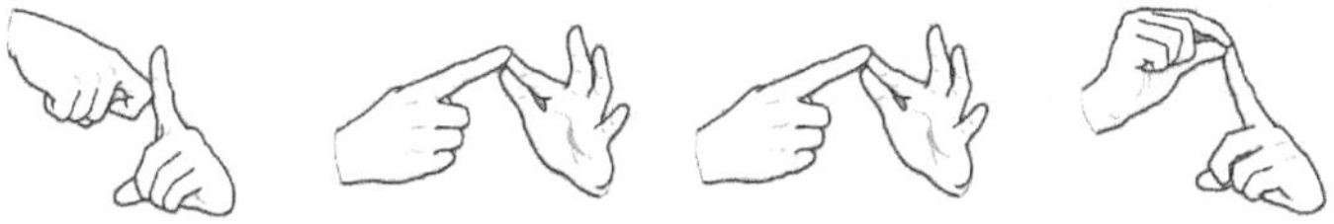

KEEP CALM AND SIGN

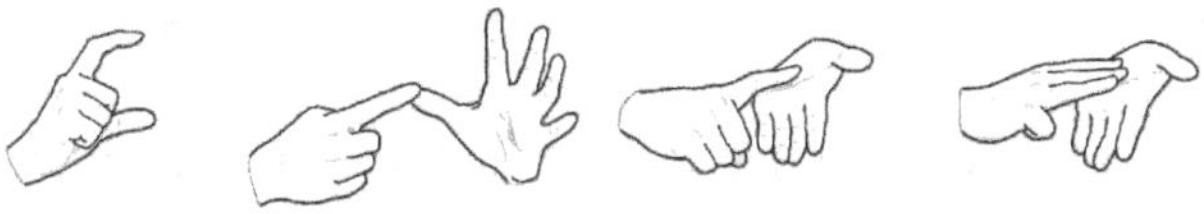

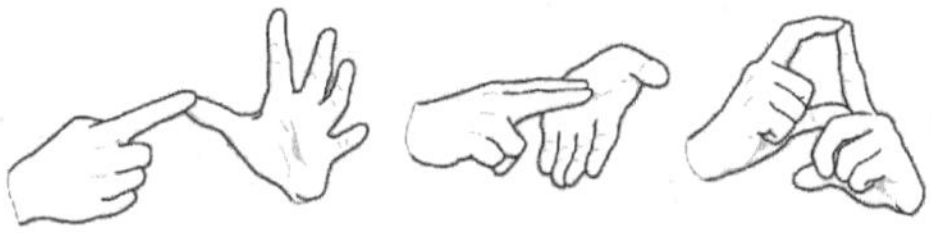

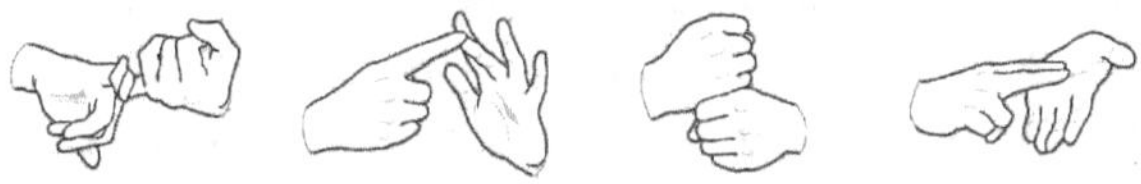

CRISTIE PUBLISHING

© Copyright 2022-2025- All rights reserved.

You may not reproduce, duplicate or send the contents of this book without direct written permission from the author. You cannot hereby despite any circumstance blame the publisher or hold him or her to legal responsibility for any reparation, compensations, or monetary forfeiture owing to the information included herein, either in a direct or an indirect way.

Legal Notice: This book has copyright protection. You can use the book for personal purpose. You should not sell, use, alter, distribute, quote, take excerpts or paraphrase in part or whole the material contained in this book without obtaining the permission of the author first.

Disclaimer Notice: You must take note that the information in this document is for casual reading and entertainment purposes only. We have made every attempt to provide accurate, up to date and reliable information. We do not express or imply guarantees of any kind. The persons who read admit that the writer is not occupied in giving legal, financial, medical or other advice. We put this book content by sourcing various places.

Please consult a licensed professional before you try any techniques shown in this book. By going through this document, the book lover comes to an agreement that under no situation is the author accountable for any forfeiture, direct or indirect, which they may incur because of the use of material contained in this document, including, but not limited to, ―errors, omissions, or inaccuracies.

How to sign in British Sign Language

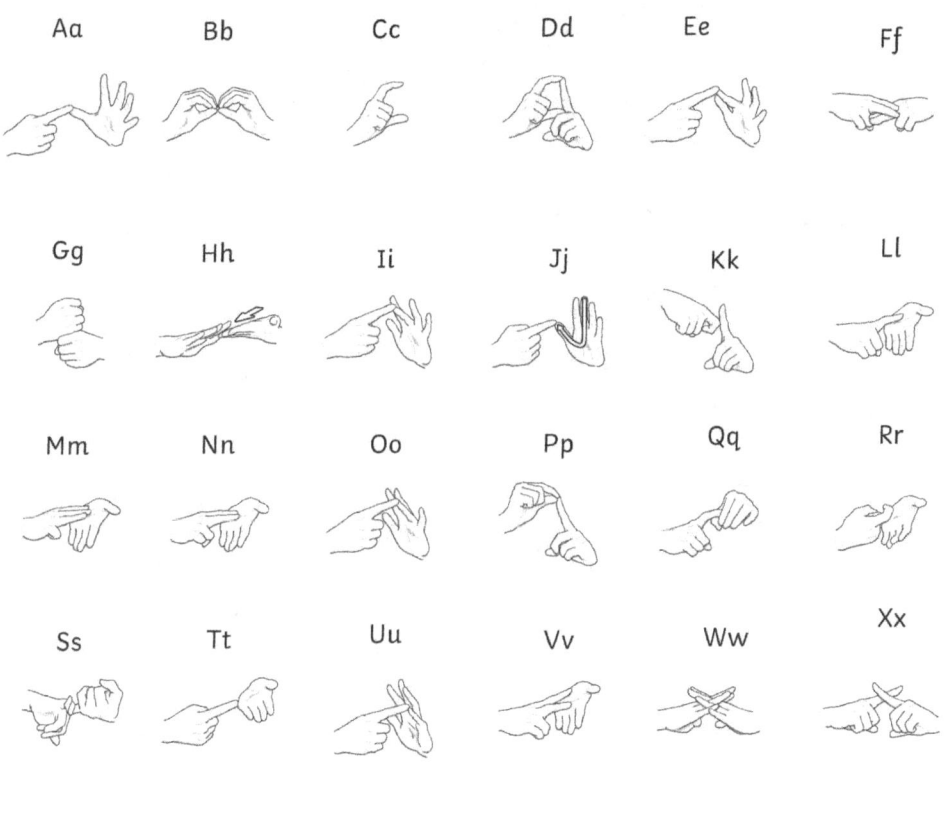

Phase 2 Sound British Sign Language Fingerspelling

s

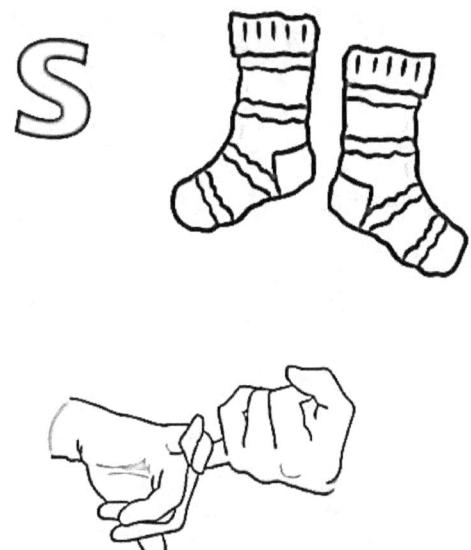

a

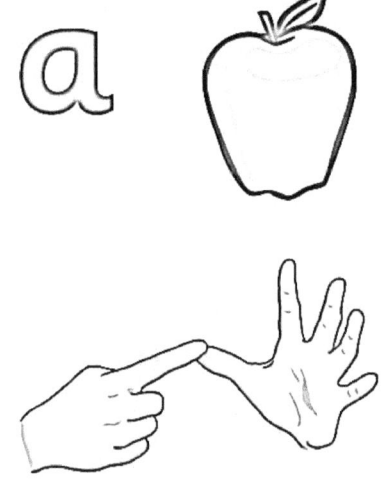

t

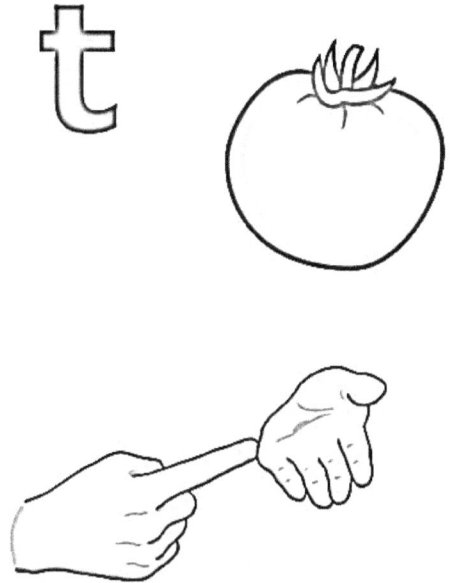

p

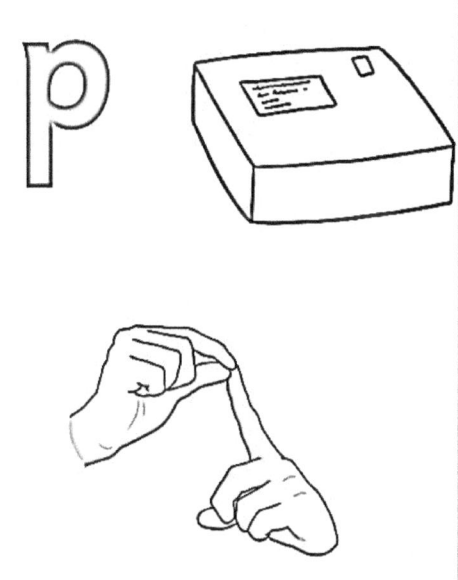

i

n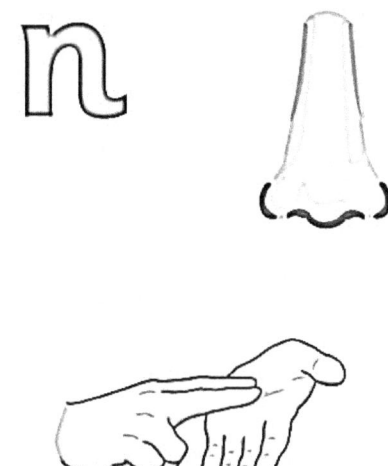

m

d

g

o

c

k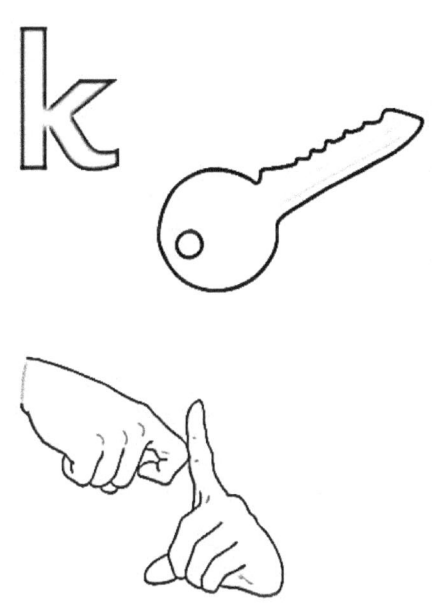

ck

e

u

r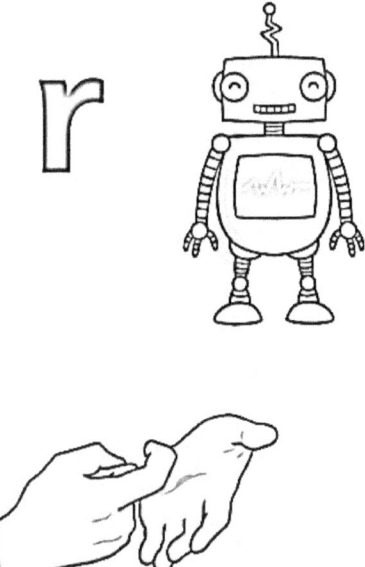

h

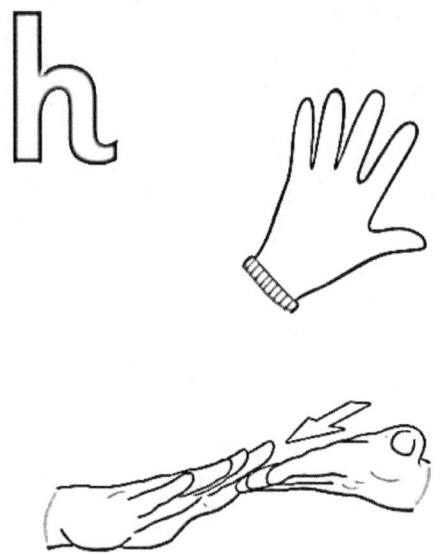

b

f

ff

l

ll

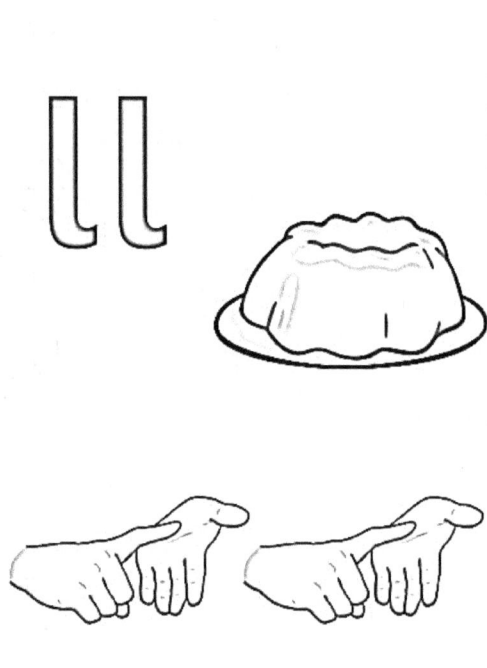

ss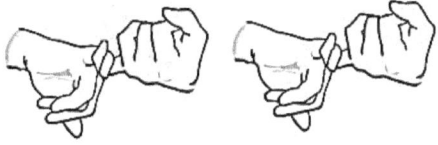

Phase 3 Sound British Sign Language Fingerspelling

j

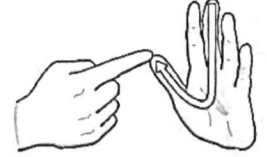

v

W

X

y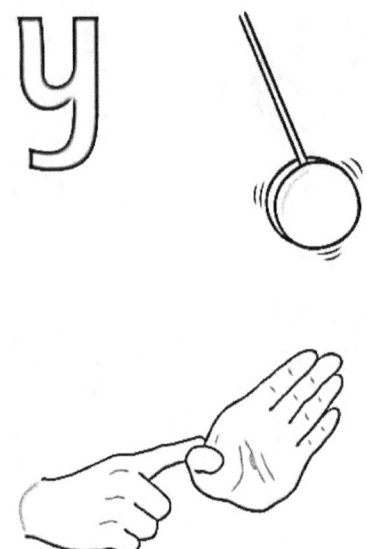

z

zz

qu

ch

sh

th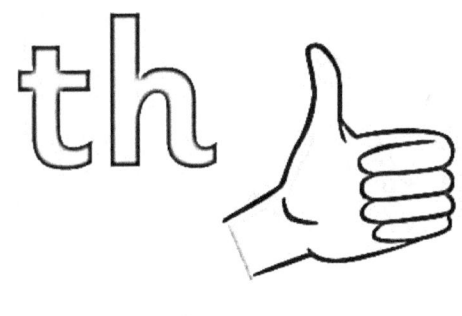

ng

ai

ee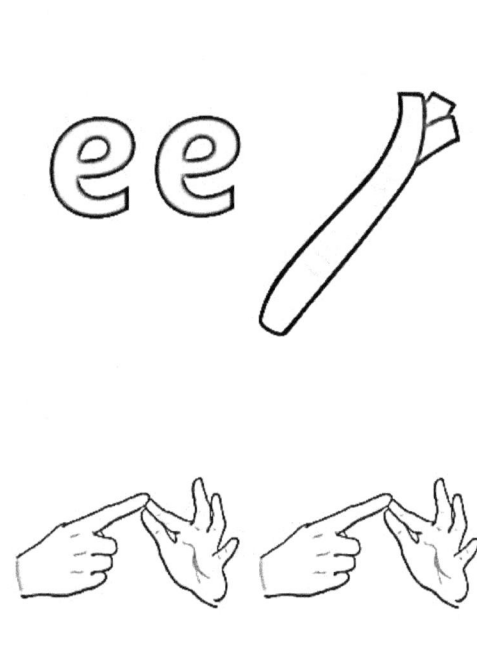

igh

oa

oo

oo

ar

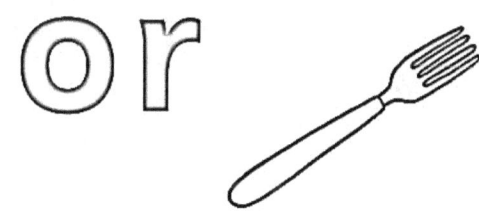

or

ur

ow

oi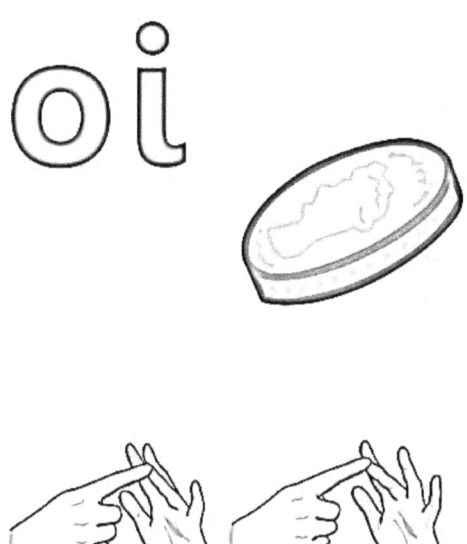

ear

air

ure

er

Phase 4 Sound British Sign Language Fingerspelling

bl

br

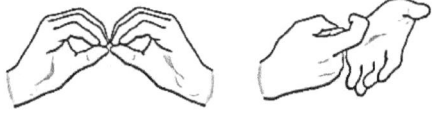

cl

cr

dr

fl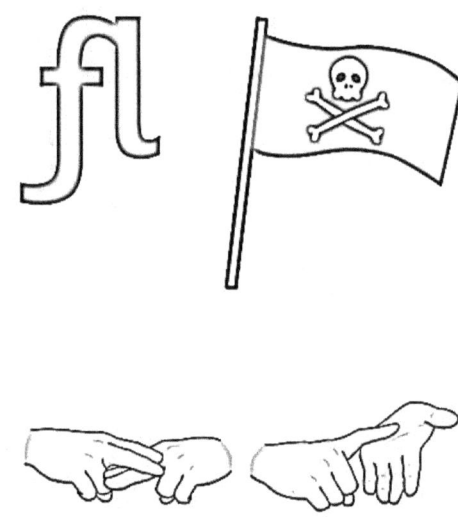

fr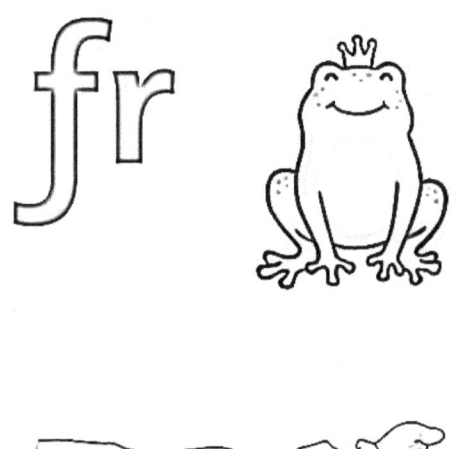

gl

gr

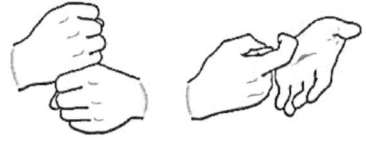

sm

sn

pl

pr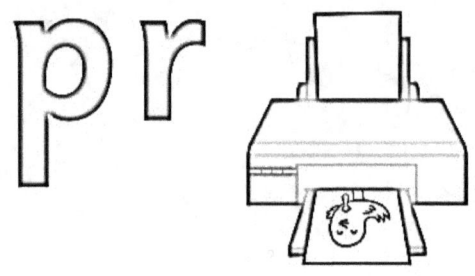

sc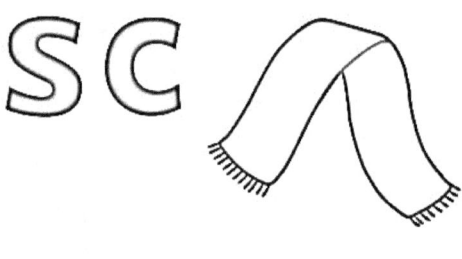

scr

shr

sk

sl

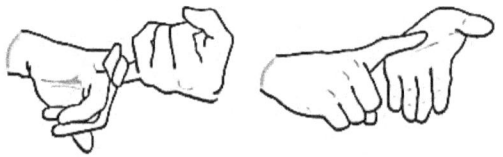

sp
st

str

thr

tr

tw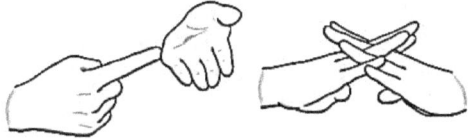

Phase 5 sound British Sign Language Fingerspelling

ay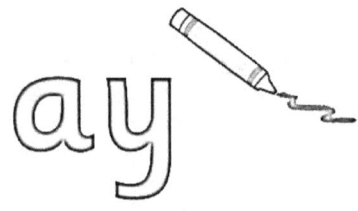

ou

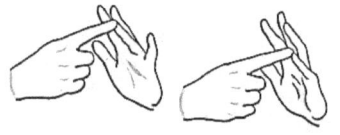

ie

oy

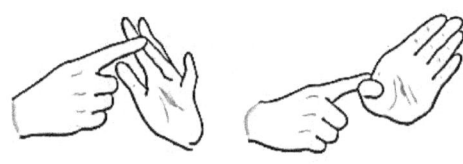

ir

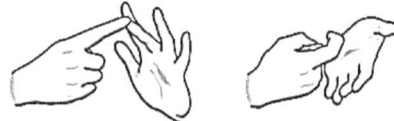

ue

ue

aw

wh

ph

ew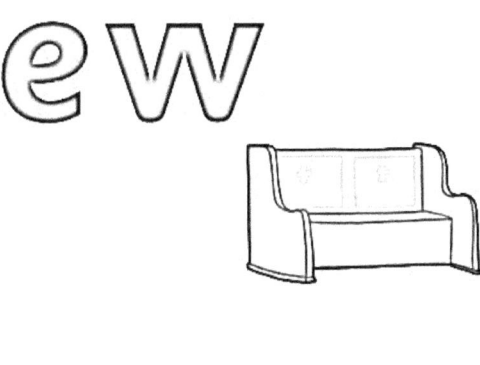

ew

oe

a u

ey

a-e

e-e

i-e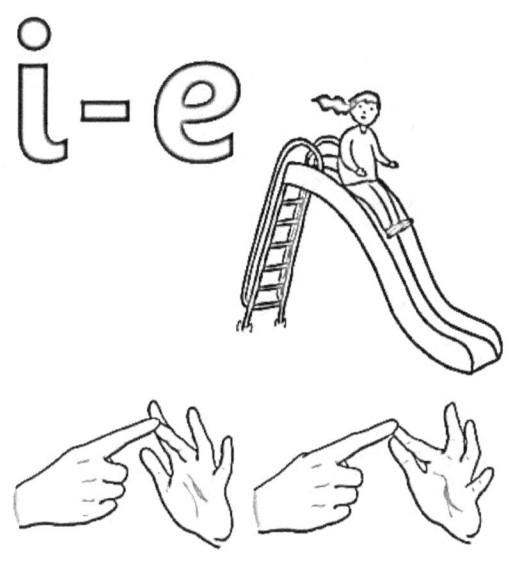

o-e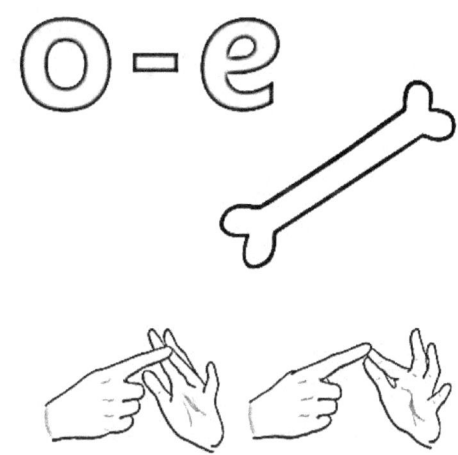

u-e

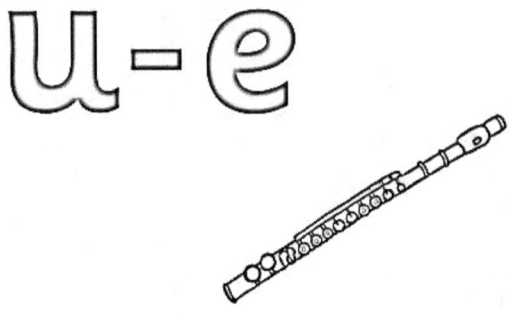

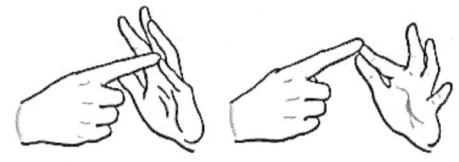

u-e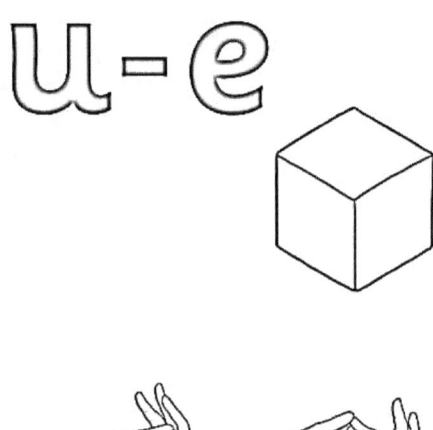

Thank you!

www.ingramcontent.com/pod-product-compliance
Lightning Source LLC
LaVergne TN
LVHW010620070526
838199LV00063BA/5213